Praying Purpose for My Life

A 13-Week Prayer Devotional Journal

International Award-Winning Author
Toneal M. Jackson

www.WeAreAPS.com

Copyright © 2020 by Toneal M. Jackson

All rights reserved.

No portion of this book may be reproduced mechanically, electronically, or by any other means, including photocopying, without written permission of the publisher.

ISBN: 978-1-945145-56-8

Author's Note

The purpose of the Prayer Devotional Journal is to lead you into a lifestyle of prayer by becoming more acquainted with God. Prayer is our way of communicating with God. More than just a moment of providing a list of demands (the things we want and need), prayer is a spiritual state of mind. It is a time where we not only speak *to* God but wait to hear *from* God.

Our prayer lives may lack substance because we don't pray on a consistent basis. Oftentimes, I've heard people say, "I don't know how to pray" or even, "I don't know what to pray." This interactive Prayer Devotional Journal is designed to teach methods of prayer. There is a weekly scripture provided, an explanation as to how the given scripture applies to you, as well as a prayer tip that can help improve your prayer life.

Week 1

Romans 8:28

"And we know that all things work together for good to them that love God, to them who are the called according to His purpose."

Explanation

If you love God and His son, Jesus, "all things" – every situation, experience, and circumstance, God will cause it all to work in your favor.

Prayer Tip

Pray for guidance so that your purpose is revealed.

Monday

How can praying for God's purpose to be revealed benefit your partner? Take time to communicate to God why you believe this request to be important for your significant other.

My prayer for my spouse (partner):

_____
_____
_____
_____
_____
_____
_____
_____
_____
_____
_____
_____
_____

Tuesday

How can praying for God's purpose to be revealed benefit your child(ren)? Take time to communicate to God why you believe this request to be important for him/her/them.

My prayer for my child(ren):

_____
_____
_____
_____
_____
_____
_____
_____
_____
_____
_____
_____

Wednesday

How can praying for God's purpose to be revealed benefit your family? Take time to communicate to God why you believe this request to be important for them.

My prayer for my family:

_____
_____
_____
_____
_____
_____
_____
_____
_____
_____
_____
_____
_____

Thursday

How can praying for God's purpose to be revealed benefit your church and pastor? Take time to communicate to God why you believe this request to be important for them.

My prayer for my church and pastor:

_____
_____
_____
_____
_____
_____
_____
_____
_____
_____
_____
_____

Friday

How can praying for God's purpose to be revealed benefit your boss/co-workers? Take time to communicate to God why you believe this request to be important for them.

My prayer for my boss/co-workers:

_____
_____
_____
_____
_____
_____
_____
_____
_____
_____
_____
_____

Saturday

How can praying for God's purpose to be revealed benefit your enemy? Take time to communicate to God why you believe this request to be important for them.

My prayer for my enemy/enemies:

_____
_____
_____
_____
_____
_____
_____
_____
_____
_____
_____
_____
_____
_____

Sunday

How can praying for God's purpose to be revealed benefit you? Take time to communicate to God why you believe this request to be important.

My prayer for myself:

_____
_____
_____
_____
_____
_____
_____
_____
_____
_____
_____
_____
_____

Week 2

Proverbs 16:4

*"The Lord has made everything for His own purposes,
even the wicked
for a day of disaster."*

Explanation

God made everything for the purpose of glorifying Him. Although everyone may not choose to do so, ultimately everyone will have no choice but to do so.

Prayer Tip

Ask God to help you abstain from being one of the wicked.

Monday

How can doing good deeds benefit your partner? Take time to communicate to God why you believe this request to be important for your significant other.

My prayer for my spouse (partner):

_____
_____
_____
_____
_____
_____
_____
_____
_____
_____
_____
_____
_____
_____

Tuesday

How can doing good deeds benefit your child(ren)? Take time to communicate to God why you believe this request to be important for him/her/them.

My prayer for my child(ren):

_____
_____
_____
_____
_____
_____
_____
_____
_____
_____
_____
_____
_____

Wednesday

How can doing good deeds benefit your family? Take time to communicate to God why you believe this request to be important for them.

My prayer for my family:

_____
_____
_____
_____
_____
_____
_____
_____
_____
_____
_____
_____
_____

Thursday

How can doing good deeds benefit your church and pastor? Take time to communicate to God why you believe this request to be important for them.

My prayer for my church and pastor:

_____
_____
_____
_____
_____
_____
_____
_____
_____
_____
_____
_____
_____

Friday

How can doing good deeds benefit your boss/co-workers? Take time to communicate to God why you believe this request to be important for them.

My prayer for my boss/co-workers:

_____
_____
_____
_____
_____
_____
_____
_____
_____
_____
_____
_____

Saturday

How can doing good deeds benefit your enemy? Take time to communicate to God why you believe this request to be important for them.

My prayer for my enemy/enemies:

_____
_____
_____
_____
_____
_____
_____
_____
_____
_____
_____
_____
_____

Sunday

How can doing good deeds benefit you? Take time to communicate to God why you believe this request to be important.

My prayer for myself:

_____
_____
_____
_____
_____
_____
_____
_____
_____
_____
_____
_____
_____
_____

Week 3

Ecclesiastes 8:6

"For there is a proper time and procedure for every matter, though a person may be weighed down by misery."

Explanation

There is an appointed time for everything in our lives to occur. Whether life, death, and all in between will happen, and bring about a range of emotions, which is natural.

Prayer Tip

Pray for understanding and the ability to accept the things that happen in your life.

Monday

How can understanding the will of God benefit your partner? Take time to communicate to God why you believe this request to be important for your significant other.

My prayer for my spouse (partner):

_____
_____
_____
_____
_____
_____
_____
_____
_____
_____
_____
_____

Tuesday

How can understanding the will of God benefit your child(ren)? Take time to communicate to God why you believe this request to be important for him/her/them.

My prayer for my child(ren):

_____
_____
_____
_____
_____
_____
_____
_____
_____
_____
_____
_____
_____

Wednesday

How can understanding the will of God benefit your family? Take time to communicate to God why you believe this request to be important for them.

My prayer for my family:

_____
_____
_____
_____
_____
_____
_____
_____
_____
_____
_____
_____
_____
_____

Thursday

How can understanding the will of God benefit your church and pastor? Take time to communicate to God why you believe this request to be important for them.

My prayer for my church and pastor:

_____
_____
_____
_____
_____
_____
_____
_____
_____
_____
_____

Friday

How can understanding the will of God benefit your boss/co-workers? Take time to communicate to God why you believe this request to be important for them.

My prayer for my boss/co-workers:

_____
_____
_____
_____
_____
_____
_____
_____
_____
_____
_____
_____
_____

Saturday

How can understanding the will of God benefit your enemy? Take time to communicate to God why you believe this request to be important for them.

My prayer for my enemy/enemies:

_____
_____
_____
_____
_____
_____
_____
_____
_____
_____
_____
_____
_____

Sunday

How can understanding the will of God benefit you? Take time to communicate to God why you believe this request to be important.

My prayer for myself:

_____
_____
_____
_____
_____
_____
_____
_____
_____
_____
_____
_____

Week 4

Isaiah 45:18

"For thus says the Lord, who created the heavens, who formed the earth and made it: I am the Lord, and there is no other."

Explanation

We must understand that there is only one Creator.
God created everything.
We must acknowledge and reference that fact.

Prayer Tip

Pray for a spirit of humility.

Monday

How can the spirit of humility benefit your partner? Take time to communicate to God why you believe this request to be important for your significant other.

My prayer for my spouse (partner):

_____
_____
_____
_____
_____
_____
_____
_____
_____
_____
_____
_____
_____
_____

Tuesday

How can the spirit of humility benefit your child(ren)? Take time to communicate to God why you believe this request to be important for him/her/them.

My prayer for my child(ren):

_____
_____
_____
_____
_____
_____
_____
_____
_____
_____
_____
_____
_____

Wednesday

How can the spirit of humility benefit your family? Take time to communicate to God why you believe this request to be important for them.

My prayer for my family:

_____
_____
_____
_____
_____
_____
_____
_____
_____
_____
_____
_____
_____

Thursday

How can the spirit of humility benefit your church and pastor? Take time to communicate to God why you believe this request to be important for them.

My prayer for my church and pastor:

_____
_____
_____
_____
_____
_____
_____
_____
_____
_____
_____
_____

Friday

How can the spirit of humility benefit your boss/co-workers? Take time to communicate to God why you believe this request to be important for them.

My prayer for my boss/co-workers:

_____
_____
_____
_____
_____
_____
_____
_____
_____
_____
_____
_____
_____

Saturday

How can the spirit of humility benefit your enemy? Take time to communicate to God why you believe this request to be important for them.

My prayer for my enemy/enemies:

_____
_____
_____
_____
_____
_____
_____
_____
_____
_____
_____
_____
_____
_____

Sunday

How can the spirit of humility benefit you? Take time to communicate to God why you believe this request to be important.

My prayer for myself:

_____
_____
_____
_____
_____
_____
_____
_____
_____
_____
_____
_____
_____
_____

Week 5

2 Timothy 2:25

"Gently instruct those who oppose the truth. Perhaps God will change those people's hearts, and they will learn the truth."

Explanation

Try to educate
those who don't know.
Pray that God will open their eyes
and give them an ear to hear,
and a heart to receive.

Prayer Tip

Pray for patience.

Monday

How can having patience benefit your partner? Take time to communicate to God why you believe this request to be important for your significant other.

My prayer for my spouse (partner):

_____
_____
_____
_____
_____
_____
_____
_____
_____
_____
_____
_____
_____

Tuesday

How can having patience benefit your child(ren)? Take time to communicate to God why you believe this request to be important for him/her/them.

My prayer for my child(ren):

_____
_____
_____
_____
_____
_____
_____
_____
_____
_____
_____
_____

Wednesday

How can having patience benefit your family? Take time to communicate to God why you believe this request to be important for them.

My prayer for my family:

_____
_____
_____
_____
_____
_____
_____
_____
_____
_____
_____
_____
_____

Thursday

How can having patience benefit your church and pastor? Take time to communicate to God why you believe this request to be important for them.

My prayer for my church and pastor:

_____
_____
_____
_____
_____
_____
_____
_____
_____
_____
_____
_____
_____
_____

Friday

How can having patience benefit your boss/co-workers? Take time to communicate to God why you believe this request to be important for them.

My prayer for my boss/co-workers:

_____
_____
_____
_____
_____
_____
_____
_____
_____
_____
_____
_____
_____

Saturday

How can having patience benefit your enemy? Take time to communicate to God why you believe this request to be important for them.

My prayer for my enemy/enemies:

_____
_____
_____
_____
_____
_____
_____
_____
_____
_____
_____
_____
_____

Sunday

How can having patience benefit you? Take time to communicate to God why you believe this request to be important.

My prayer for myself:

_____
_____
_____
_____
_____
_____
_____
_____
_____
_____
_____
_____
_____
_____

Week 6

Genesis 1:31

"And God saw everything that He had made, and behold, it was very good. And the evening and the morning were the sixth day."

Explanation

God has taken the time to create everything. He took to acknowledge that everything He made was very good. Since you are God's creation, He sees you as being very good.

Prayer Tip

Pray that God allows you to see yourself the way that He sees you.

Monday

How can seeing using the eyes of God benefit your partner? Take time to communicate to God why you believe this request to be important for your significant other.

My prayer for my spouse (partner):

_____
_____
_____
_____
_____
_____
_____
_____
_____
_____
_____
_____
_____

Tuesday

How can seeing using the eyes of God benefit your child(ren)? Take time to communicate to God why you believe this request to be important for him/her/them.

My prayer for my child(ren):

_____
_____
_____
_____
_____
_____
_____
_____
_____
_____
_____
_____
_____
_____

Wednesday

How can seeing using the eyes of God benefit your family? Take time to communicate to God why you believe this request to be important for them.

My prayer for my family:

_____
_____
_____
_____
_____
_____
_____
_____
_____
_____
_____
_____

Thursday

How can seeing using the eyes of God benefit your church and pastor? Take time to communicate to God why you believe this request to be important for them.

My prayer for my church and pastor:

_____
_____
_____
_____
_____
_____
_____
_____
_____
_____
_____
_____
_____
_____

Friday

How can seeing using the eyes of God benefit your boss/co-workers? Take time to communicate to God why you believe this request to be important for them.

My prayer for my boss/co-workers:

_____
_____
_____
_____
_____
_____
_____
_____
_____
_____
_____
_____
_____
_____

Saturday

How can seeing using the eyes of God benefit your enemy? Take time to communicate to God why you believe this request to be important for them.

My prayer for my enemy/enemies:

_____
_____
_____
_____
_____
_____
_____
_____
_____
_____
_____
_____
_____

Sunday

How can seeing using the eyes of God benefit you? Take time to communicate to God why you believe this request to be important.

My prayer for myself:

_____
_____
_____
_____
_____
_____
_____
_____
_____
_____
_____
_____
_____

Week 7

Joshua 24:15

"And if it seem evil to you to serve the Lord, choose for yourselves this day whom you will serve. But as for me and my house, we will serve the Lord."

Explanation

Serving God is a
personal decision;
no one can make it for you.
Be deliberate in choosing
to serve God.

Prayer Tip

Pray for clarity.

Monday

How can making intentional decisions benefit your partner? Take time to communicate to God why you believe this request to be important for your significant other.

My prayer for my spouse (partner):

_____
_____
_____
_____
_____
_____
_____
_____
_____
_____
_____

Tuesday

How can making intentional decisions benefit your child(ren)? Take time to communicate to God why you believe this request to be important for him/her/them.

My prayer for my child(ren):

_____
_____
_____
_____
_____
_____
_____
_____
_____
_____
_____
_____
_____

Wednesday

How can making intentional decisions benefit your family? Take time to communicate to God why you believe this request to be important for them.

My prayer for my family:

_____
_____
_____
_____
_____
_____
_____
_____
_____
_____
_____
_____

Thursday

How can making intentional decisions benefit your church and pastor? Take time to communicate to God why you believe this request to be important for them.

My prayer for my church and pastor:

_____
_____
_____
_____
_____
_____
_____
_____
_____
_____
_____
_____
_____
_____

Friday

How can making intentional decisions benefit your boss/co-workers? Take time to communicate to God why you believe this request to be important for them.

My prayer for my boss/co-workers:

_____
_____
_____
_____
_____
_____
_____
_____
_____
_____
_____
_____

Saturday

How can making intentional decisions benefit your enemy? Take time to communicate to God why you believe this request to be important for them.

My prayer for my enemy/enemies:

_____
_____
_____
_____
_____
_____
_____
_____
_____
_____
_____
_____
_____

Sunday

How can making intentional decisions benefit you? Take time to communicate to God why you believe this request to be important.

My prayer for myself:

_____
_____
_____
_____
_____
_____
_____
_____
_____
_____
_____
_____

Week 8

Hebrews 4:12

"For the word of God is alive and active. Sharper than any double-edged sword, it penetrates even to dividing soul and spirit, joints and marrow; it judges the thoughts and attitudes of the heart."

Explanation

We are to be obedient to the word of God. We are to walk in our purpose as God has created us to do so as not to be separated from God.

Prayer Tip

Pray that God strengthens you to walk in your purpose.

Monday

How can being obedient to the word of God benefit your partner? Take time to communicate to God why you believe this request to be important for your significant other.

My prayer for my spouse (partner):

_____
_____
_____
_____
_____
_____
_____
_____
_____
_____
_____
_____

Tuesday

How can being obedient to the word of God benefit your child(ren)? Take time to communicate to God why you believe this request to be important for him/her/them.

My prayer for my child(ren):

_____
_____
_____
_____
_____
_____
_____
_____
_____
_____
_____
_____
_____

Wednesday

How can being obedient to the word of God benefit your family? Take time to communicate to God why you believe this request to be important for them.

My prayer for my family:

_____
_____
_____
_____
_____
_____
_____
_____
_____
_____
_____
_____
_____

Thursday

How can being obedient to the word of God benefit your church and pastor? Take time to communicate to God why you believe this request to be important for them.

My prayer for my church and pastor:

_____
_____
_____
_____
_____
_____
_____
_____
_____
_____
_____
_____
_____

Friday

How can being obedient to the word of God benefit your boss/co-workers? Take time to communicate to God why you believe this request to be important for them.

My prayer for my boss/co-workers:

_____
_____
_____
_____
_____
_____
_____
_____
_____
_____
_____
_____
_____

Saturday

How can being obedient to the word of God benefit your enemy? Take time to communicate to God why you believe this request to be important for them.

My prayer for my enemy/enemies:

_____
_____
_____
_____
_____
_____
_____
_____
_____
_____
_____
_____

Sunday

How can being obedient to the word of God benefit you? Take time to communicate to God why you believe this request to be important.

My prayer for myself:

_____
_____
_____
_____
_____
_____
_____
_____
_____
_____
_____
_____
_____

Week 9

1 Corinthians 14:12

*"So, it is with you. Since you are eager for gifts of the Spirit,
try to excel in those
that build up the church."*

Explanation

Use the gifts that you possess
to help edify and
encourage others – especially
those that are within
the body of Christ.

Prayer Tip

Ask God to show you how to use your gift(s) to help others.

Monday

How can helping others benefit your partner? Take time to communicate to God why you believe this request to be important for your significant other.

My prayer for my spouse (partner):

_____
_____
_____
_____
_____
_____
_____
_____
_____
_____
_____
_____
_____

Tuesday

How can helping others benefit your child(ren)? Take time to communicate to God why you believe this request to be important for him/her/them.

My prayer for my child(ren):

_____
_____
_____
_____
_____
_____
_____
_____
_____
_____
_____
_____
_____
_____

Wednesday

How can helping others benefit your family? Take time to communicate to God why you believe this request to be important for them.

My prayer for my family:

_____
_____
_____
_____
_____
_____
_____
_____
_____
_____
_____
_____
_____

Thursday

How can helping others benefit your church and pastor? Take time to communicate to God why you believe this request to be important for them.

My prayer for my church and pastor:

_____
_____
_____
_____
_____
_____
_____
_____
_____
_____
_____
_____
_____

Friday

How can helping others benefit your boss/co-workers? Take time to communicate to God why you believe this request to be important for them.

My prayer for my boss/co-workers:

_____
_____
_____
_____
_____
_____
_____
_____
_____
_____
_____
_____
_____

Saturday

How can helping others benefit your enemy? Take time to communicate to God why you believe this request to be important for them.

My prayer for my enemy/enemies:

_____
_____
_____
_____
_____
_____
_____
_____
_____
_____
_____
_____
_____
_____

Sunday

How can helping others benefit you? Take time to communicate to God why you believe this request to be important.

My prayer for myself:

_____
_____
_____
_____
_____
_____
_____
_____
_____
_____
_____
_____
_____
_____

Week 10

Philippians 2:13

*"For God is working in you,
giving you the desire
and the power
to do what pleases Him."*

Explanation

God gives us gifts that we can use to glorify Him. Our gifts are not to be used solely for personal satisfaction; we should desire to help others and please God.

Prayer Tip

Praying for the spirit of selflessness.

Monday

How can the spirit of selflessness benefit your partner? Take time to communicate to God why you believe this request to be important for your significant other.

My prayer for my spouse (partner):

_____
_____
_____
_____
_____
_____
_____
_____
_____
_____
_____
_____
_____
_____

Tuesday

How can the spirit of selflessness benefit your child(ren)? Take time to communicate to God why you believe this request to be important for him/her/them.

My prayer for my child(ren):

_____
_____
_____
_____
_____
_____
_____
_____
_____
_____
_____
_____
_____

Wednesday

How can the spirit of selflessness benefit your family? Take time to communicate to God why you believe this request to be important for them.

My prayer for my family:

_____
_____
_____
_____
_____
_____
_____
_____
_____
_____
_____
_____

Thursday

How can the spirit of selflessness benefit your church and pastor? Take time to communicate to God why you believe this request to be important for them.

My prayer for my church and pastor:

_____
_____
_____
_____
_____
_____
_____
_____
_____
_____
_____
_____
_____
_____

Friday

How can the spirit of selflessness benefit your boss/co-workers? Take time to communicate to God why you believe this request to be important for them.

My prayer for my boss/co-workers:

_____
_____
_____
_____
_____
_____
_____
_____
_____
_____
_____
_____
_____

Saturday

How can the spirit of selflessness benefit your enemy? Take time to communicate to God why you believe this request to be important for them.

My prayer for my enemy/enemies:

_____
_____
_____
_____
_____
_____
_____
_____
_____
_____
_____
_____
_____
_____

Sunday

How can the spirit of selflessness benefit you? Take time to communicate to God why you believe this request to be important.

My prayer for myself:

_____
_____
_____
_____
_____
_____
_____
_____
_____
_____
_____
_____

Week 11

2 Corinthians 9:7

*"So, let each one give as
he purposes in his heart,
not grudgingly or of necessity;
for God loves a cheerful giver."*

Explanation

Whatever you do or give, let it be from a place of sincerity.
Doing something just so that others can see you, or simply to satisfy someone else won't benefit you if your heart isn't in the right place.

Prayer Tip

Ask God to allow your deeds to be rooted in joy and sincerity.

Monday

How can possessing joy benefit your partner? Take time to communicate to God why you believe this request to be important for your significant other.

My prayer for my spouse (partner):

_____
_____
_____
_____
_____
_____
_____
_____
_____
_____
_____
_____

Tuesday

How can possessing joy benefit your child(ren)? Take time to communicate to God why you believe this request to be important for him/her/them.

My prayer for my child(ren):

_____
_____
_____
_____
_____
_____
_____
_____
_____
_____
_____
_____
_____

Wednesday

How can possessing joy benefit your family? Take time to communicate to God why you believe this request to be important for them.

My prayer for my family:

_____
_____
_____
_____
_____
_____
_____
_____
_____
_____
_____
_____

Thursday

How can possessing joy benefit your church and pastor? Take time to communicate to God why you believe this request to be important for them.

My prayer for my church and pastor:

_____
_____
_____
_____
_____
_____
_____
_____
_____
_____
_____
_____
_____
_____
_____

Friday

How can possessing joy benefit your boss/co-workers? Take time to communicate to God why you believe this request to be important for them.

My prayer for my boss/co-workers:

_____
_____
_____
_____
_____
_____
_____
_____
_____
_____
_____
_____

Saturday

How can possessing joy benefit your enemy? Take time to communicate to God why you believe this request to be important for them.

My prayer for my enemy/enemies:

_____
_____
_____
_____
_____
_____
_____
_____
_____
_____
_____
_____
_____
_____

Sunday

How can possessing joy benefit you? Take time to communicate to God why you believe this request to be important.

My prayer for myself:

_____
_____
_____
_____
_____
_____
_____
_____
_____
_____
_____
_____
_____

Week 12

Job 42:2

*"I know that You (Lord) can do
everything, and that
no purpose of Yours
can be withheld from You."*

Explanation

There is nothing that is
too hard for God to do.
When we acknowledge that He
is the reason that everything exists,
He will bless us.

Prayer Tip

*Acknowledge God and His
goodness.*

Monday

How can acknowledging the goodness of God benefit your partner? Take time to communicate to God why you believe this request to be important for your significant other.

My prayer for my spouse (partner):

Tuesday

How can acknowledging the goodness of God benefit your child(ren)? Take time to communicate to God why you believe this request to be important for him/her/them.

My prayer for my child(ren):

_____
_____
_____
_____
_____
_____
_____
_____
_____
_____
_____
_____
_____

Wednesday

How can acknowledging the goodness of God benefit your family? Take time to communicate to God why you believe this request to be important for them.

My prayer for my family:

_____
_____
_____
_____
_____
_____
_____
_____
_____
_____
_____
_____
_____

Thursday

How can acknowledging the goodness of God benefit your church and pastor? Take time to communicate to God why you believe this request to be important for them.

My prayer for my church and pastor:

_____
_____
_____
_____
_____
_____
_____
_____
_____
_____
_____
_____

Friday

How can acknowledging the goodness of God benefit your boss/co-workers? Take time to communicate to God why you believe this request to be important for them.

My prayer for my boss/co-workers:

_____
_____
_____
_____
_____
_____
_____
_____
_____
_____
_____
_____

Saturday

How can acknowledging the goodness of God benefit your enemy? Take time to communicate to God why you believe this request to be important for them.

My prayer for my enemy/enemies:

_____
_____
_____
_____
_____
_____
_____
_____
_____
_____
_____
_____
_____
_____

Sunday

How can acknowledging the goodness of God benefit you? Take time to communicate to God why you believe this request to be important.

My prayer for myself:

_____
_____
_____
_____
_____
_____
_____
_____
_____
_____
_____
_____

Week 13

Exodus 9:16

"But indeed, for this purpose I have raised you up, that I may show My power in you, and that My name may be declared in all the earth."

Explanation

The reason you exist is so that God can be glorified. Regardless of the respective gift or talent, you were ultimately created so that people can see and know God.

Prayer Tip

Accept God's will and purpose for your life.

Monday

How can acceptance of God's will benefit your partner? Take time to communicate to God why you believe this request to be important for your significant other.

My prayer for my spouse (partner):

_____
_____
_____
_____
_____
_____
_____
_____
_____
_____
_____
_____
_____
_____
_____

Tuesday

How can acceptance of God's will benefit your child(ren)? Take time to communicate to God why you believe this request to be important for him/her/them.

My prayer for my child(ren):

_____
_____
_____
_____
_____
_____
_____
_____
_____
_____
_____
_____
_____

Wednesday

How can acceptance of God's will benefit your family? Take time to communicate to God why you believe this request to be important for them.

My prayer for my family:

_____
_____
_____
_____
_____
_____
_____
_____
_____
_____
_____
_____
_____
_____

Thursday

How can acceptance of God's will benefit your church and pastor? Take time to communicate to God why you believe this request to be important for them.

My prayer for my church and pastor:

_____
_____
_____
_____
_____
_____
_____
_____
_____
_____
_____
_____
_____
_____

Friday

How can acceptance of God's will benefit your boss/co-workers? Take time to communicate to God why you believe this request to be important for them.

My prayer for my boss/co-workers:

_____
_____
_____
_____
_____
_____
_____
_____
_____
_____
_____
_____
_____
_____

Saturday

How can acceptance of God's will benefit your enemy? Take time to communicate to God why you believe this request to be important for them.

My prayer for my enemy/enemies:

_____
_____
_____
_____
_____
_____
_____
_____
_____
_____
_____
_____
_____

Sunday

How can acceptance of God's will benefit you? Take time to communicate to God why you believe this request to be important.

My prayer for myself:

_____
_____
_____
_____
_____
_____
_____
_____
_____
_____
_____
_____
_____

Epilogue

The hope is that now that you have reached the end of this journal, you have learned:

- That prayer is not just about you
- How to pray more effectively
- How to seek God for your purpose

I also pray that you have obtained a greater sense of purpose than you possessed 13 weeks ago. My desire is that you have a clearer understanding of why you were created. Remember, whenever life tries to confuse you, trust God and seek Him for clarity.

Toneal M. Jackson is a National and International Award-Winning Author; Publisher; and Inspirational Speaker. She is the founder of Artists Promoting Success, as well as #ImGladToBeAWoman, an organization that empowers women.

In 2012, CBS Chicago named her one of "5 Indie Authors and Publishers to Watch Out For". She was inducted into the Young Women's Professional League in 2016 and POWER (Professional Organization of Women of Excellence Recognized) in 2018. In 2019, she received the I Change Nations Award for her work in the literary industry. For more on Toneal, visit: www.AWEInspiringCoach.com

Other Books by Toneal M. Jackson:

Pleasing Your Partner: A Spiritual Guide to H.A.P.P.I.N.E.S.S.
Four Girls: A Lot of Choices
Four Girls Learn Their Colors
It's A Way to Say It All: How to Communicate with Your Kids
It's A Way to Say It All: How to Communicate with Your Partner
Growing Up to be Happy
She's Out. I'm In
Inspiration from A.B.O.V.E.
Learning to Love Me
Love Me...Please
Being an Authorpreneur: How to Succeed in the Book Business
The Race to the Ring: The Seven Cs of a Successful Courtship
The Fruit of the Spirit Anthology:
Taking Life's Bitter Moments and Making Them Sweet
Praying Peace for My Life (Journal)
Praying Problems out of My Life (Journal)
Praying Prosperity into My Life (Journal)
Praising through the Pandemic

www.ingramcontent.com/pod-product-compliance
Lightning Source LLC
LaVergne TN
LVHW051846080426
835512LV00018B/3090